A GLIMPSE INTO MY MIND

KATRINNA R. HUDSON

To my late mother Darcie Leann Pablo-Hudson

Thank you for teaching me to never give up on my dreams

Contents

1. Darkness with in the clouds

The sky is dark with very litte clouds

It smells like Autumn rain, you hear thunder but you can't figure out where it's coming from

You sit and stare waiting to see the droplets fall like the clouds are crying

The thunder gets louder and then you see the light

Raindrops pour down like a morning shower and the darkness creeps in like a freightened child waiting for the storm to pass; but the darkness doesn't

The rain slows down like life does at the end of the night and you realize why there's darkness in the clouds

2. Lavender

The way she wore Lavender it became my favorite smell like
Spring time with a little bit of love written in it's cracks
The way she smelled like Cherry Blossoms made my world
stop as if it was only her and I in that moment but when the
smell faded away along with her smile I realized I only loved
Lavender when she wore it
Everytime I smell the sweetness of the Sweetpea my teeth hurt
as if it was only her that brought meaning to the smell
The day I realized it was over was when the Lavender faded
and my aching in my teeth went away, when my world kept
spinning when I smelled the Cherry Blossom
My heart fluttered when I saw her but she wore a new scent,
one I didn't recognize and that's how I knew she was no longer
mine

3. Hostage

They say time heals all wounds but when I find a photo of you
the wounds break free as if I held them prisoner

The wounds open as if I was just a vessel they used to store
their anger

The wounds are not the prisoners they are the guards and I am
the hostage in my own body held at gunpoint with a loaded
two syllable sentence of "she's gone"

The screams echoing in my brain like the screams of the
soldiers that lay in the battlefield

These wounds are not the prisoners they are the guards and I
am the only hostage

4. The Numbers On The Scale

They said growing up the higher the number on the scale meant that I was growing the way I was supposed to but when I was 12 years old looking seven months pregnant they told me to eat less and so when I ate less the numbers on the scale went down and everyone was proud of me

Freshman year of highschool and the numbers on the scale fell, 210 205 200 195

Sophmore year the weight piled back on 210 215 220

Junior year and the numbers on the scale continued to get higher 220 225 230 240 250

Senior year I stopped eating and the numbers fell drastically 250 240 230

my depression had come to light and consumed within the darkness my mind had created I had no will to take care of myself but the numbers on the scale came back even higher than the years prior

I stopped eating but the numbers never fell 4 years later and years of recovery, the numbers finally stayed the same

5. Reality

He told us you were gone and I didn't want to believe him

I scream and cried hoping that you'd hear me and come running back but 8 years later and my heart still shatters everyday waiting for you to say "it was all a joke, I'm sorry come over and I'll explain"

I whispered your name in hopes you'd hear me

I screamed and I begged but you didn't come back

I longed to feel your arms around me just for a minute and when that minute passed, I begged for another minute I begged for another hour

I begged for all the reasons just for you to never return back to me and so when I laid there trying to grasp reality by the strings of what seemed impossible, I realized you never left, I just can't see you

6. I love you

I love you; that's what we say never love you because the "I" before the love is so much more important

Because love you is a statement but I love you is a reminder

A reminder that even when the days are rough and the nights are dark and the sun no longer shines and the light in your eyes has grown dim I love you is a reminder that no matter what happens I'm not going anywhere

Where love you is a dead statement surrounded but the pungent smell of uneasiness

Where love you is already a broken heart ready to break some more

A love you is full of empty promises and dead wishes

I love you is a reminded

Love you is a statement

But when nights got too rough and the tide too high the I love yous became love yous and when the wind blew everything in a storm of chaos the I love yous became love yous

When the sun was drowned by the waves of sadness that once took over my beating heart the I love yous became love yous and love yous were filled with empty promises and so when I begged you to love me, you told me you couldn't anymore

I remember the last I love you but I also remember the last love you

7. Ages

17, that's the number in which I was touched for the without my permission the first time

17 that was the age in which I feared men, feeling used, disgusted and angry

19 was the number in which a boy I barely knew tried to get me to have sex with him

19 was the age in which I could never look at myself the same feeling disgusted once again

I felt ashamed, weak, unheard questioning everything from that night

My body felt like it was my fault unable to see myself as who I was

19 was the age in which I felt like I had to show my body to men to get attionion

19 was the number in which my body count had been higher than I had every thought

22 was the age in which I still blamed myself for what happened

22 was the number in which I realized it was never my fault

8. Losing You

Days turned to weeks
Weeks turned to months
Months turned to years
Years turned to deacades
who knew that losing you would hurt more than the 206
bones I have in my body
who knew that losing you would hurt more than the burning
liquor I put into my body monhths after you left
who knew that losing you would sting more than the cutsd I
place upon my wrists and thighs
who knew that losing you would feel like I'm drowning in a
world where everyone is breathing fine
who knew that losing you would had felt like I had died too

9. Loving you was the easiest thing I had ever done

Loving you was the easiest thing I had ever done but when I laid in bed with tears upon my cheeksI knew it was no longer love I was feeling for you

My heart was heavy and I realized I loved the thought of being loved by you

You said all the right things but you showed me you didn't love me when your words never matched with your actions and for that I blame myself because I was blinded by the love you gave me once upon a time ago

I was in love with the image of you I had created in my head; the image of you where I had you by my side

But when I realized I was just a pastime, I was confused because your words seemed so full of love yet the way you treated me showed me otherwise

Loving you was the eaiest thing I had ever done, but it was also the hardest

10. Life Without You

I alway wondered what life was like without you, but now I live it

I have no choice but to sit in silence and remember everything we have ever done together

It's been almost 9 years and everyday I am haunted by the memories in which I can hear you faintly laugh

I am haunted by your mesmerizing smile and the way you call my name

Almost 9 years later and I still sit by the phone in hopes I would see your name upon my screen but I am disappointed everytime

They say time heals all wounds but it seems like everyday they reopen

Greif doesn't have a time period it enters like an unwanted guest

Coming in from the shadows like a thunderstorm getting ready to brew

I wondered what life was like without you, if only I had knew

Your eyes are the background in which my dreams have played on screens

I have to live my life without you and suddenly my heart starts to scream